Earth-Friendly Energy

Gillian Gosman

PowerKiDS press
New York

Published in 2011 by The Rosen Publishing Group, Inc.
29 East 21st Street, New York, NY 10010

First Edition

Editor: Joanne Randolph
Book Design: Kate Laczynski

Photo Credits: Cover © www.iStockphoto.com/Brian Jackson; p. 4 Comstock/ Thinkstock; pp. 5, 10, 14, 16, 17, 20 (bottom), 22–23, 26, 27 Shutterstock.com; p. 6 © www.iStockphoto.com/Jaap Hart; p. 7 Newsmakers/Getty Images; pp. 8, 11, 15, 18, 19 iStockphoto/Thinkstock; pp. 9, 21 Hemera/Thinkstock; pp. 12–13 John Foxx/Stockbyte/Thinkstock; p. 20 (top) Jupiterimages/Comstock/Thinkstock; pp. 24–25 Jupiterimages/Photos.com/Thinkstock; p. 28 Mike Harrington/Getty Images; p. 29 Saeed Khan/AFP/Getty Images; p. 30 Jupiterimages/Polka Dot/Thinkstock.

Library of Congress Cataloging-in-Publication Data

Gosman, Gillian.
 Earth-friendly energy / by Gillian Gosman. — 1st ed.
    p. cm. — (How to be Earth friendly)
 Includes index.
 ISBN 978-1-4488-2587-5 (library binding) — ISBN 978-1-4488-2763-3 (pbk.) — ISBN 978-1-4488-2764-0 (6-pack)
 1. Renewable energy resources—Juvenile literature. 2. Green technology—Juvenile literature. I. Title.
 TJ808.2.G67 2011
 333.79'4—dc22

                          2010032820

Manufactured in the United States of America

CPSIA Compliance Information: Batch #WW11PK: For Further Information contact Rosen Publishing, New York, New York at 1-800-237-9932

CONTENTS

What Is Earth-Friendly Energy?......................4

Nonrenewable Energy 7

The Power of the Sun 9

Blowing in the Wind 12

Rivers, Waves, and Tides........................ 15

Hot! Hot! Hot! 19

Fuel from the Farm 21

Nuclear Energy: Clean and Green?............. 24

Earth-Friendly Energy at Home 27

Why Don't We Just Use It? 29

Glossary 31

Index 32

Web Sites.. 32

What Is Earth-Friendly Energy?

This is a coal mine in Pennsylvania. Coal is a nonrenewable resource. Mining also hurts the land around the mine.

People today use lots of energy every day. We count on electricity to give us light and heat. We use gas to power the cars we drive. We burn fossil **fuels** to create much of this power. Fossil fuels are **natural resources** created deep under Earth's surface over millions of years. Oil, gas, coal, and petroleum are the most common fossil fuels. They are called nonrenewable resources because

Offshore oil rigs, such as this one, drill into the ocean floor for oil and natural gas. Many people are hurt on oil rigs. Oil spills from the rigs hurt the environment, too.

People have been using the power of the Sun, the wind, and water for thousands of years. This windmill uses the power of water to grind grain.

we use them up much faster than nature can produce them. They are also not **sustainable** resources because when we drill or mine them from the ground, we hurt Earth.

The power of a river, the Sun, and the wind can be gathered, used, and gathered again. This energy, or power, is sustainable. When we use it, we do not hurt nature or make harmful waste. We keep Earth healthy. For this reason, sustainable energy is also called Earth-friendly or green energy.

For hundreds of years, humans have taken advantage of Earth's rich supply of fossil fuels. In that time, we have used up most of the resources it took many millions of years to create. Some day these natural resources will be hard to find or gone altogether.

Burning fossil fuels also puts harmful gases into the **atmosphere**. These gases, such as carbon dioxide, trap heat close to Earth, just like

IT'S A FACT!

Other planets have greenhouse-style atmospheres. Venus's atmosphere keeps the planet at 900° F (482° C). Mars's thin atmosphere keeps it at -220° F (-140° C). Humans could not live in either of these places!

The hole in the ozone layer is the purple spot here. It lets more of the Sun's rays reach Earth. Earth's temperature is now getting hotter at a much faster rate than it should.

Along with warmer temperatures, climate change brings more hurricanes and tornadoes. The number of severe hurricanes each year has doubled since the 1990s.

the glass roof of a greenhouse. Some of this warmth, called the greenhouse effect, is good for the planet. However, scientists have discovered that too many of these gases in the atmosphere is causing Earth to get warmer. This is called **global warming**. This is why Earth-friendly energy is so important. It could save our planet!

Tornadoes, such as this one, cause a lot of harm to people and property. There have been more tornadoes since our climate has started getting warmer more quickly.

You can collect your own solar energy. Let the sun shine through your windows on a sunny winter day. The solar power will warm your room!

Solar power is the power of the Sun. One way it is gathered is by using solar panels, or boards. Solar panels are made from a metal called silicon. It can be cut into small, flat pieces called **photovoltaic cells**.

Photovoltaic solar panels come in all shapes and sizes. They can be set in rows in a field or fixed to the roof of a

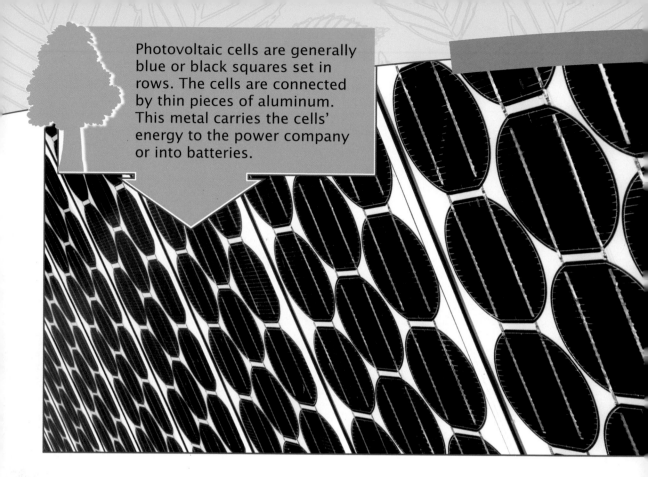

Photovoltaic cells are generally blue or black squares set in rows. The cells are connected by thin pieces of aluminum. This metal carries the cells' energy to the power company or into batteries.

house. Photovoltaic cells can collect direct sunlight on clear or cloudy days. They collect the sunlight that bounces off of snow, sand, or glass windows, too. Solar panels work best, though, when they can collect strong, direct sunlight for 6 to 10 hours at a time. At night and in shade, solar panels collect no energy.

Solar thermal energy is another way to use the Sun's power. Solar thermal energy is energy made by collecting the Sun's heat using water, stone, trapped air, or other materials. Solar thermal energy is used to do all kinds of work, such as heating and cooling buildings, cooking, and cleaning drinking water.

This house has solar panels on its roof. Power from the panels can be stored so that the power can be used even when the Sun is not shining.

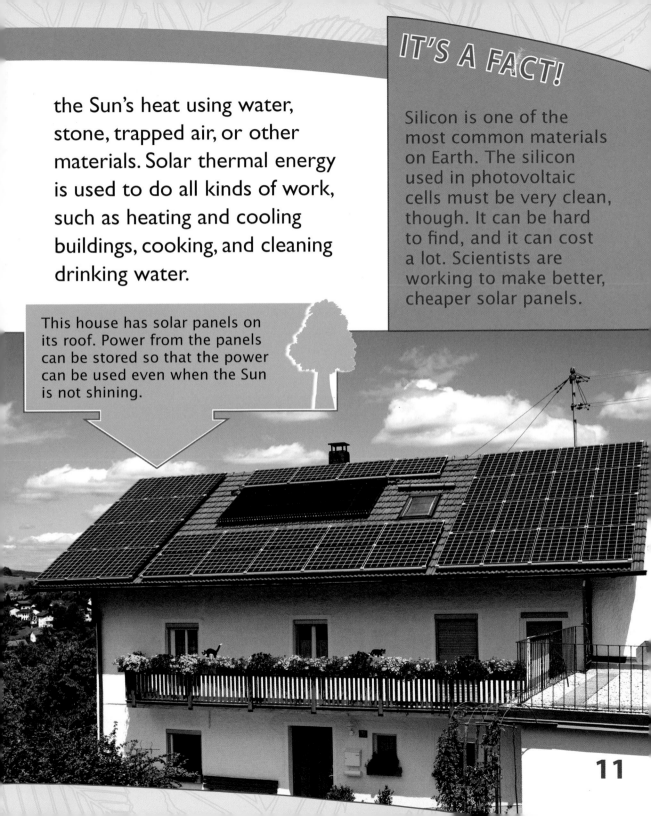

11

Blowing in the Wind

The sky is the limit when it comes to wind power! There are many ways to gather and use the wind. Wind **turbines** turn the power of the wind into electricity. Windmills use the wind's strength to work the moving parts in machines. Wind pumps move water using the power of the wind. While the

At the top of each wind turbine tower, there is a propeller with long arms that turn in the wind. The propeller connects to a turbine that creates electricity when it spins.

wind may not blow all the time, it will never run out. It is a great Earth-friendly energy source!

There is a lot of interest in building wind farms. A wind farm is a group of wind turbines. There may be several dozen or several hundred towers in a

IT'S A FACT!

In 2008, wind farms in the United States made about 52 billion kilowatt hours of electricity. This may sound like a lot, but it added up to just 1.3 percent of the total electricity produced in the country.

Use the wind at home! Hang your wet laundry on a line to dry rather than run an electric dryer! Your family will save energy and money.

Each blade on a wind turbine tower can be between 65 and 150 feet (20–46 m) long!

farm. The turbines connect to the local power company's electric system, which carries electricity to homes, businesses, and streetlights.

Wind farms are being built across the United States, Asia, Africa, Europe, Australia, and on the North Pole and South Pole. They are not always popular, though. Some people do not like the way they look. Other people argue that they make very little power and are costly to build and run.

Rivers, Waves, and Tides

Hydropower is the power of water. **Hydroelectric** dams are used to make energy from the flow of a river. A dam is a wall that blocks the flow of water. The water pools in a **reservoir** on one side of the dam. A small place at the bottom lets some of the water from the reservoir

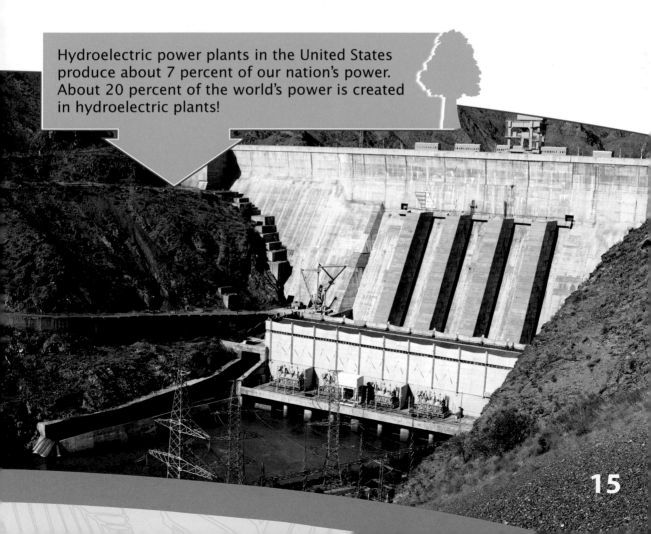

Hydroelectric power plants in the United States produce about 7 percent of our nation's power. About 20 percent of the world's power is created in hydroelectric plants!

through. There is a lot of **pressure** as the water tries to fit through the small space. This turns the blades of a turbine. The turbine changes the power of the water's movement into electricity.

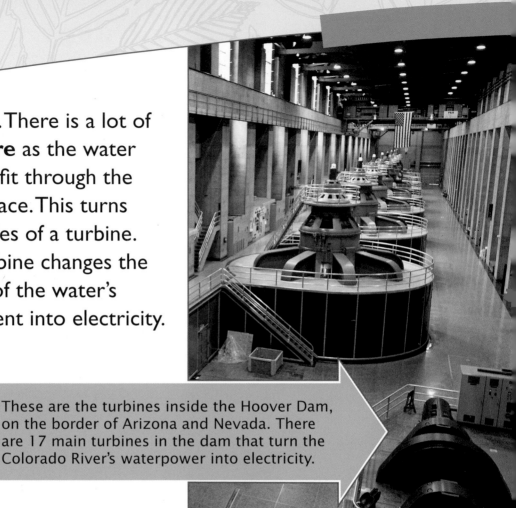

These are the turbines inside the Hoover Dam, on the border of Arizona and Nevada. There are 17 main turbines in the dam that turn the Colorado River's waterpower into electricity.

Hydroelectric dams make little waste, are cheap to run, and can make large amounts of power. They upset nature's balance, though. When a dam is built, the reservoir floods large areas of land.

Wave power can be gathered in many different ways. Some wave power systems use the power of the flowing

water to turn the blades of a turbine. Others use buoys, or floating objects, to collect the pressure created by each wave.

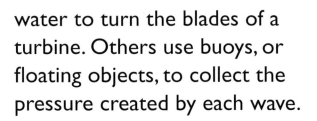

Here China's Three Gorges Dam is releasing water into the Yangtze River after using it to make electricity. The dam has done many good things, but it has hurt people and nature, too.

17

Here you can see the reservoir at the top of the Hoover Dam. The Hoover Dam produces about 4.2 billion kilowatt hours of electricity each year.

The tide is the regular rise and fall of ocean waters. Twice every day, the water level rises or falls, depending on the position of Earth and the Moon. Turbines or dams are used to collect and use the energy of the tides.

Hot! Hot! Hot!

The word "geothermal" comes from the Greek words for "Earth" and "heat." Geothermal energy uses heat from deep inside Earth to power homes and businesses.

Earth is made up of iron, rock, and **magma**. Earth's rocky outer layer is called the crust. The crust is broken into large

This is a geothermal power plant, which uses steam from deep under ground to make electricity. The steam turns a turbine just as water does in a hydroelectric plant.

pieces called plates. Where two plates meet, magma, hot water, and steam break through the crust. This makes volcanoes, hot springs, and geysers, which heat the groundwater in the crust. This water can be used for bathing, cooking, and heating buildings. Elsewhere, Earth's heat stays hidden under ground. To find it, scientists drill deep into Earth. Water and steam from beneath the ground can be piped to the top to run geothermal power plants.

Hot springs (top) and geysers (bottom) are two examples of places where Earth's heat has come to the surface.

Biofuels are liquid fuels made from organic, or living, material. The two most common kinds of biofuels are ethanol and biodiesel. Ethanol is a kind of alcohol.

It is made through fermentation, which is a way of breaking down a natural material. Corn and sugarcane are the most common kinds of natural material used in making ethanol today. Scientists are working on ways to use all kinds of plants to make biofuels. Biodiesel is made by mixing an alcohol, such as methanol, with cooking oil, vegetable oil, or animal fat.

Corn is the plant most commonly used to make biofuel in the United States. Corn takes a lot of space to grow, though.

This is an ethanol plant in South Dakota that uses corn to make its product. Many people think that ethanol is not Earth friendly, even though it is a renewable fuel source.

Ethanol and biodiesel can be mixed with gasoline to help cars run better and cleaner. Carmakers are also working to build cars that run on biofuel alone. People like that cars using biofuels release, or let go of, less carbon dioxide than cars running on just gasoline.

People worry that there are other costs for nature, though. For example, to grow the corn for ethanol, farmers must clear land, use **pesticides** that dirty nearby waterways, and create other harmful waste.

Nuclear Energy: Clean and Green?

Everything in our world is made up of **atoms**. This includes your school, your fingernails, and the air you breathe. Nuclear power is created by breaking an atom in two. Splitting an atom is called **nuclear fission**. When the atom is split, heat is released. In a nuclear power plant, that heat warms water, turning it into steam. The steam powers turbines that make electricity.

Some people believe that nuclear power is clean and green, or Earth friendly. Nuclear power plants do not release carbon dioxide, as do power plants that

Have you ever seen a nuclear power plant? The round buildings on this plant are cooling towers. The turbines are in the rectangular buildings behind them.

There are 68 nuclear power plants in the United States. They make about 20 percent of the electricity we use.

run on fossil fuels. However, nuclear power plants do make another kind of waste called radioactive waste. Each split atom is radioactive, meaning it is unstable, or easy to break apart. Radioactive energy is harmful to humans.

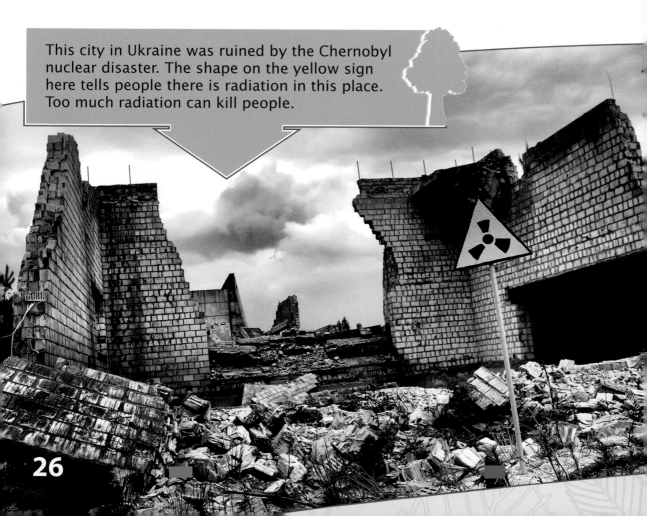

This city in Ukraine was ruined by the Chernobyl nuclear disaster. The shape on the yellow sign here tells people there is radiation in this place. Too much radiation can kill people.

Earth-Friendly Energy at Home

This business uses Earth-friendly solar panels to power itself. You can help the environment by visiting businesses that use power made from renewable resources.

Many of the Earth-friendly energy sources in this book can be bought and used at home, at school, and by businesses. More and more people are using solar cells and wind turbines to help power, heat, and cool buildings.

You can also cut back on the energy you use. You can do this by turning off machines that run on electricity when they are not being used. You can also set the temperature in your house a few degrees cooler in winter and warmer in summer. Use natural light and heat as much as you can and switch to energy-saving lightbulbs, too. Use gasoline-powered cars only when you have to. Walk or ride a bicycle when possible.

Riding bikes with your family instead of driving helps the environment. It is fun, too!

Why Don't We Just Use It?

Green energy **technology** has come a long way. It still faces problems, though. First, solar cells, wind turbines, hydroelectric dams, biofuels, and other Earth-friendly

Earth's health is important. Governments around the world have been holding many meetings to talk about ways we can all work together to save our environment.

energy systems are expensive! It costs money to make the machines that gather the energy, set them in place, connect them to the power company, and repair them when needed. Many of these machines do not work as

In 1997, 187 countries signed the Kyoto Protocol and agreed to lower the amount of greenhouse gases they released. Other international plans to keep the planet healthy are in the works, too.

Hanging your laundry to dry instead of using a clothes dryer saves energy. Can you think of other ways to help Earth?

well as they may someday. This just means that, today, they waste some of the energy that they gather.

Communities, businesses, and countries around the world are coming together to make better green energy technology. Perhaps the first step is making sure everyone understands how important Earth-friendly energy is to the health of our planet!

GLOSSARY

atmosphere (AT-muh-sfeer) The gases around an object in space. On Earth this is air.

atoms (A-temz) The smallest parts of elements that can exist either alone or with other elements.

fuels (FYOO-elz) Things that are used to make energy, warmth, or power.

global warming (GLOH-bul WAWRM-ing) A gradual increase in how hot Earth is. It is caused by gases that are let out when people burn fuels such as gasoline.

hydroelectric (hy-droh-ih-LEK-trik) Having energy that is created by flowing water.

magma (MAG-muh) A hot liquid rock underneath Earth's surface.

natural resources (NA-chuh-rul REE-sors-ez) Things in nature that can be used by people.

nuclear fission (NOO-klee-ur FIH-shun) The way an atom is split in two to create power.

pesticides (PES-tuh-sydz) Poisons used to kill pests.

photovoltaic cells (foh-toh-vol-TAY-ik SELZ) Flat objects that collect sunlight and change it into electricity.

pressure (PREH-shur) A force that pushes on something.

reservoir (REH-zuh-vwar) A stored body of water.

sustainable (suh-STAY-nuh-bel) Able to be kept going.

technology (tek-NAH-luh-jee) The way that people do something using tools and the tools that they use.

turbines (TER-bynz) Machines in which water, wind, or steam moves blades to make electricity.

INDEX

A
atmosphere, 7–8
atom(s), 24, 26

D
dam(s), 15–16, 18, 29

F
fuels, 4, 7, 21, 26

G
global warming, 8

M
magma, 19–20

N
natural resources, 4, 7
nuclear fission, 24

P
photovoltaic cells, 9–10
pressure, 16–17

R
reservoir, 15–16

T
technology, 29–30
turbine(s), 12, 14, 16–18,
    24, 27, 29

WEB SITES

Due to the changing nature of Internet links, PowerKids Press has developed an online list of Web sites related to the subject of this book. This site is updated regularly. Please use this link to access the list:
www.powerkidslinks.com/hbef/energy/